CLASSIC NORTH AMERICAN STEAM

NILS HUXTABLE

SMITHMARK

This edition published
by SMITHMARK Publishers Inc.
16 East 32nd Street
New York, New York 10016

SMITHMARK books are available for bulk purchase for sales promotion and premium use. For details write or telphone the Manager of Special Sales, SMITHMARK Publishers Inc., 16 East 32nd Street, New York, NY 10016, (212) 532 6600.

Produced by Brompton Books Corp.,
15 Sherwood Place,
Greenwich, CT 06830

ISBN 0-8317-1474-3

Printed in Hong Kong

10 9 8 7 6 5 4

Reprinted 1993

Page 1: No 19 of the Oregon, Pacific & Eastern leads an excursion past Dorena Lake in Oregon. *Pages 2-3:* Bound for Summit, Wisconsin, Western Coal & Coke No 1 doubleheads with Saginaw Timber No 2. *These pages:* Leaving a billow of smoke behind it, Union Pacific's 4-6-6-4 Challenger No 3985 charges across the gently rolling foothills of the West.

All photos by Nils Huxtable unless otherwise noted.

Contents

Introduction	6	The 2-8-4 Berkshire/2-10-4 Texas	84
The 4-4-0 American	8	The 4-8-2 Mountain	88
The 4-4-2 Atlantic	10	The 4-8-4 Northern	92
The 0-6-0 Switcher	12	The 2-6-6-2 Articulated	108
The 2-6-0 Mogul	18	The 2-6-6-4 Articulated	112
The 2-6-2 Prairie	24	The 4-6-6-4 Challenger	116
The 4-6-0 Ten-wheeler	30	The Shay	120
The 4-6-2 Pacific	42	The Heisler	124
The 4-6-4 Hudson	50	The Climax	126
The 2-8-0 Consolidation	54	Index	128
The 2-8-2 Mikado	64	Bibliography	128

INTRODUCTION

An era ended in 1960, when the major railroads in the United States and Canada dieselized. Having served the continent for more than a century, North America's most visible symbol of industrial supremacy was obsolete. In railroad yards everywhere, thousands of steam engines stood gathering rust or waiting silently in their roundhouse stalls for an emergency call to service. Reinstatement, even a temporary one, never came: a recession, the accompanying decrease in traffic and an abundance of new diesel power made sure of that.

Indeed, the commitment to advanced technology was so complete that the management of most railroads wanted nothing to do with nostalgia, and most of the surviving steam locomotives—some of them recently rolled out—were sold for a fraction of their true value and unceremoniously cut up for scrap. A few were donated to parks and museums, but, even so, such historically significant classes as the New York Central's Niagaras met the torch. Some railroads—for whom profit was far more important than preservation and the past something to be obliterated rather than cherished—could not be bothered to save even one steam locomotive for posterity. Certain railfan extremists may be justified in holding the view that such companies, whose names have since been lost to mergers over the years, are hardly worth remembering.

Still, rather than mourn what is gone, it is better to appreciate what remains. We can be grateful that a handful of railroads went out of their way not only to preserve part of their heritage but to continue operating steam locomotives long after the cost of overhauling and maintenance had become an extravagance. Tribute is owed to such railroads as the Union Pacific and the Southern (now Norfolk Southern), who felt a steam locomotive was a more effective public relations tool at the head of a train than behind a chain link fence. The author well remembers his first steam excursion: a trip from Denver to Laramie behind 4-8-4 No 8444—the only steam locomotive in North America never to be officially retired. That was 30 years ago. These days, the UP and Norfolk Southern are still in the forefront of main line steam operation, and other railroads—among them Conrail and Southern Pacific—are eager to join the club.

The increase in the number of main line steam excursions in recent years has been paralleled by a flourishing of tourist railroads and museums. On a few miles of track, smaller steam locomotives—2-6-0s, 2-8-0s, Ten-wheelers—and geared engines

are put through their paces, providing passengers with an earful of bells and whistles for a nominal charge. In California, for example, where main line steam after 1958 was anathema to the principal railroads serving the state, the Sierra Railway became a shrine for enthusiasts in need of a whiff of smoke, hot steam and lubricating oil. Everything remains in its original condition, and steam trains are once again whistling their way through the foothills of the Mother Lode.

In certain instances, however, restoration of steam locomotives has been less than satisfying, especially for those who remember them in regular service. Alas, some tourist lines hold the philosophy that the real thing is just not good enough. Gaudy paint schemes, 'old time' smokestacks, headlights, cowcatchers and, more recently, plates and plaques advertising the locomotive's sponsorship have been added in what can be termed the 'Petticoat Junction' approach to preserving railroad history, or what noted railroad authority Ron Zeil has labeled 'Tasteless, Tedious and Tortured.'

Fortunately, these eyesores are the exceptions. Among preservationists and the general public alike, there is an increasing awareness that a steam locomotive need only be itself to arouse fascination and draw a crowd. With a degree of selectivity, an album such as this can show many examples of accurate restoration that illustrate the development of steam locomotives while evoking the mood of this exciting period in North American history. Thus, worthy organizations such as the Mid-Continent Railway Museum at North Freedom, Wisconsin, which have resisted the temptation of crass commercialism, are given extensive coverage. The author still recalls his first glimpse of the museum's Chicago & Northwestern 4-6-0 charging through the autumn foliage of Wisconsin. It captured the feeling of branch line railroading as it once was, free from fakery or tomfoolery. Here, then, are a few glimpses of the North American steam scene as it is today. The dedication and enthusiasm of those involved in steam preservation—many of them volunteers—have helped to make these photographs possible. May Jamestown and North Freedom and the steam programs of Union Pacific and Norfolk Southern live on as a legacy to future generations.

Opposite: No 28 of the Sierra Railway serves as a reminder of the glorious days of steam.

The 4-4-0 American

For fifty years, the American, or Eight-wheeler, enjoyed widespread popularity as the predominant locomotive on the North American continent. The swivel four-wheel leading truck made the 4-4-0 well-suited to the steep grades, severe curvature and primitive roadbed of railroads in the mid-nineteenth century. With widely spaced wheels, the American was easy to maintain and repair, but a narrow firebox limited its hauling capacity and the increasingly heavy trains of the 1900s required larger locomotives, such as the 4-6-2 Pacific. By 1900, construction of new 4-4-0s had almost ceased, but not before a grand total of 25,000 had been turned out by such manufacturers as Rogers, Baldwin, Cooke and Mason.

On the *opposite page* is the famous *Inyo*, built in 1875 by Burnham, Parry, Williams and Company (later Baldwin) for the Virginia & Truckee Railroad. Used by Paramount Pictures in many movies between 1938 and 1968, the *Inyo* now resides at the Nevada State Railroad Museum in Carson City.

One of the oldest operating 4-4-0s in Canada is former Canadian Pacific Railway No 22, supplied by Dubs and Company of Scotland in 1882. Sold in 1918 to City of Winnipeg Hydro to become their No 3, the 4-4-0 remained in regular service until the early 1960s. During the summer months, the engine hauls tourist trains for the Prairie Dog Central. Both the No 3, owned by the Vintage Locomotive Society, and the *Inyo* are seen *below*, side by side at Vancouver's Steamexpo.

Among the last 4-4-0s built was Pennsylvania Railroad No 1223 *(right)*, which emerged from the Pennsy's own Juniata Shops in 1905. Donated to the Railroad Museum of Pennsylvania in 1979, the 1223 is a regular performer on the Strasburg Railroad.

The 4-4-2 Atlantic

A 4-4-2 built in 1896 for the Atlantic City Railroad gave the wheel arrangement its name. The two-wheel trailing truck supported a larger firebox, resulting in a passenger locomotive that was powerful as well as fast. The most remarkable Atlantics of all were those built by Alco for the Milwaukee Road's *Hiawatha* in 1935. Fitted with air-smooth shrouds, these streamlined speedsters could top 100 miles per hour with ease. Unfortunately, none were preserved.

An Atlantic that still sees occasional use, however, is the Railroad Museum of Pennsylvania's No 8063. This locomotive carries the identity of a more famous classmate, No 7002—which in 1905 was credited with a maximum speed of 127.1 miles per hour. The original was scrapped, and the 8063 is its stand-in. Doublehead-ing with 4-4-0 No 1223, the replacement 7002 *(below)* represents the classic turn-of-the-century 4-4-2. Longer trains of heavy-weight steel cars were beyond their hauling capacity, and the more powerful Pacifics relegated most Atlantics to suburban service.

Also on display at the Railroad Museum of Pennsylvania is one of the Pennsy's large-boilered E6 Class Atlantics: No 460 *(opposite)*, built in 1914. This engine hauled a two-coach 'Flyer' from Washington to New York, carrying news footage of aviator Charles Lindbergh's return from Paris in 1927.

Eighty E6s were built, making a grand total of 573 Pennsylvania Railroad 4-4-2s. Later employed on New Jersey commuter trains, No 460 and other E6s lasted into the 1950s.

The 0-6-0 Switcher

The 0-6-0 type was more widespread in Europe than in North America, where it was generally limited to switching duties. Even so, large numbers were built in the United States and Canada, and the very last steam locomotives constructed for a US railroad were 0-6-0 switchers that emerged from the Norfolk & Western Railroad's Roanoke factory in 1953. Small driving wheels and a small firebox and boiler characterized most of these engines.

Coal-fired 4466 *(these pages)* is one of the 'Harriman Standard' designs adopted by both the Union Pacific and Southern Pacific railroads. Built by Lima, the 4466 was among the last in a series of similar engines delivered to the UP in 1920. After working in Cheyenne, Wyoming, and Grand Island, Nebraska, for most of its career, the powerful switcher was donated to the California State Railroad Museum in Sacramento.

Although the 4466 usually hauls a train of passenger cars, museum staff kindly consented to the photographer's request for a 'caboose hop'. The resulting picture shows the 0-6-0 in a more authentic pose, reminiscent of the days when the 4466 was still earning its keep for the mighty UP.

One of the smaller 'goats' that once switched yards and factories across the continent is Northern Pacific E-9 Class 0-6-0 No 1070 *(below)*, built by Alco in 1907. Taken out of service in 1959, this was the NP's last active steamer. Today, the 1070 belongs to the Culp family and operates on their Lake Whatcom Railway, near Wickersham, Washington.

Saddle- and side-tank 0-6-0s were also built. Typical of the group is Great Western's 0-6-0 ST No 3 *(below)*, a 1928 Porter that was used to position hoppers of sugar beets at the company's plant in Billings, Montana. No 3 was one of the few steam locomotives to see revenue service in North America in the 1980s. The two principal Canadian railroads—the Canadian Pacific Railway and Canadian National—acquired large numbers of 0-6-0s. Former CNR No 7312 was built by Baldwin for the Grand Trunk Railway in 1908. After various renumberings, the locomotive became a member of Class 0-9a and survived until the end of steam in Canada. It is now on the Strasburg Railroad's roster as their No 31 *(opposite)*.

The 2-6-0 Mogul

The first 2-6-0, or Mogul, appeared in France in 1841, but it was not until the 1860s, when North American builders began turning out 2-6-0s en masse, that the type came into its own in the United States and Canada as a general service locomotive. Between 1860 and 1910, no fewer than 11,000 Moguls were built. In practice, 2-6-0s were assigned to freights, but despite their relatively small driving wheels, they could exceed their accepted maximum speed limit of 50 miles per hour when used on light passenger trains. The Moguls became useful branch line engines when larger, more powerful locomotives of the 2-8-0 Consolidation type ousted them from main line duties.

Dardanelle & Russellville No 9 (below) was built by Baldwin for the Cincinnati, New Orleans & Texas Railroad Company. The diminutive 2-6-0, now part of the Mid-Continent Railroad Museum's meticulously restored collection at North Freedom, Wisconsin, is seen heading a train along the branch to Quartzite.

In the picture opposite, No 9 takes water from the wooden water tank in the North Freedom yard. Such scenes were once commonplace in rural areas of North America, where the country branch line served as an important link with the outside world. Though the D & R itself is now history, No 9's cab and tender still carry the initials of that backwoods Arkansas railroad.

D & R No 9 *(opposite)*—doubleheading with Chicago & Northwestern Ten-wheeler No 1385—looks puny by comparison, yet it puts on an impressive show while helping the 4-6-0 pull a passenger train of heavyweight equipment upgrade near Summit, Wisconsin.

A much larger Mogul and another Baldwin graduate is Southern Pacific Class M-6 No 1744 *(below)*, one of the numerous 2-6-0s saved by the railroad and donated to cities along its route as the steam era came to a close. On display at Corrine, Utah from 1959 until 1981, the 1744 now leads a more useful existence: hauling passengers on the Heber Creeper, located at Heber City, Utah.

Southern Pacific owned 355 Moguls, some of which transferred their lines south of the Rio Grande; these engines remained in Mexico City after 1951 when the Mexican government assumed control of SP's operations there.

Another view of the 1744 *(these pages)* shows the engine nearing the end of its run at Charleston, Utah. Projects to restore at least two more Southern Pacific Moguls have been considered.

24

The 2-6-2 Prairie

I n North America, the 2-6-2, or Prairie, did not find favor with Class I railroads, either as a passenger engine or a freight hog. Only 1500 Prairies were built. Many went to short lines such as the Sierra Nevada Wood & Lumber Company, which purchased No 8 *(these pages)* as a woodburner from Baldwin in 1907. Converted to oil firing, the little engine had three more owners before becoming Feather River Short Line Railroad

No 8, in which guise it was restored by members of the Feather River Short Line Society and other museum volunteers at Portola, California, in 1987, at their own expense. When these pictures were taken, No 8 was the main attraction at the Portola Railroad Museum, where former Western Pacific engineer Jim Boynton obliged with some spectacular smoke effects for the benefit of visiting photographers.

Another short line serving the Feather River region was the Quincy Railroad, which bought Prairie tank No 2 *(below)* from Alco in 1924. Placed on standby when a diesel arrived on the property twenty years later, No 2 eventually became part of the Pacific Locomotive Association's collection in 1964. Today, it is a likely candidate for future operation on the group's Niles Canyon Railway near Fremont, California.

Of the four former McCloud River Railroad engines preserved, only 2-6-2 No 25 *(opposite)* remained on the premises after dieselization. Built by Alco in 1925, the engine was reactivated for excursion use and became a familiar sight in the Mount Shasta area during the 1960s, hauling trains with such unromantic names as the *Shasta Huff 'n' Puff* and the *McCloud River Rattler*. Annual snow trains were also popular.

More recent steamings of No 25 have included movie work (*Stand By Me*) and snow trains. Near the wooden water tank in Bartle, California, No 25 *(below)* makes a run-by for photographers.

The 4-6-0 Ten-Wheeler

Indisputably the best general service type of all was the 4-6-0, or Ten-wheeler. Beginning in 1850, approximately 16,000 4-6-0s were constructed. They were used in fast passenger service, on commuter trains and on slow freights. Equally comfortable on main or branch lines, the Ten-wheeler survived into the last decade of steam operation in the United States and Canada. Many 4-6-0s escaped the scrapper's torch, and a few have been restored to active duty by museum groups.

The Chicago & Northwestern Railroad employed many of its Ten-wheelers—including No 1385 (Alco 1907)—on commuter trains. These days the locomotive *(these pages)* seems quite at home on the Mid-Continent Railway at North Freedom, Wisconsin. Those former Lackawanna commuter cars may seem a bit out of place on this rural branch line, but minor details are perhaps best overlooked when the desired effect of railroading as it used to be has been achieved.

Ten-wheelers also served the narrow gauge. Looking as though it just arrived with the thrice-weekly freight from Owenyo, Southern Pacific's *Slim Princess* No 9 *(opposite)* waits at Laws, California, as it has done since 1960, when the last segment of the old Carson & Colorado closed. Built by Baldwin in 1909 for the Nevada-California-Oregon Railway, No 9 became SP's last steam locomotive to operate in regular service.

Undoubtedly the most-photographed locomotive in the world is Sierra Railway No 3 *(below)*, which has been featured in many television shows and Westerns, including the classic *High Noon*. Built as a coal-burner in 1981 by Rogers Locomotive Works for the Prescott & Arizona Central Railway, the 4-6-0 continues 'to act naturally' for the cameras of the rail buff and Hollywood director alike.

To celebrate the 1988 resumption of steam excursions on the Sierra Railway, No 3 doubleheaded with 2-8-0 No 28 *(these pages)* on the grade up Montezuma Hill, between Chinese Camp and Jamestown, California. Based at the Railtown 1897 roundhouse, both engines are favorites with railway enthusiasts, particularly those in California, where the Sierra continued to operate steam locomotives long after other railroads had dispensed with theirs.

There is no mistaking the Baldwin lineage of Nevada Northern No 40, shown *below* at East Ely, Nevada. Built in 1910, the Ten-wheeler returned to active duty in 1987, after a quarter century of storage inside the East Ely locomotive shops. Occasionally, the engine is fired up to take two wooden clerestory-roof cars over the tracks of this once bustling copper-hauling short line.

Another Baldwin, No 25 *(below)* of the Virginia & Truckee Railroad, served its owner from 1905 until 1947, when the engine was sold to RKO Radio Pictures. Now housed at the Nevada State Railroad Museum in Carson City, Nevada, No 25 is one of the many pieces of V & T equipment keeping the memory of that lost, lamented railroad alive. On selected weekends, the comely Ten-wheeler hauls three restored V & T cars around a mile-long loop of museum trackage.

Northern Pacific Class S-10 No 328 *(opposite)* was intended, not for the branch lines of Minnesota, but for the main lines of South Manchuria in China. Alco built the engine in 1905, and NP acquired it in 1907, using it primarily on branch freight and mixed train duties, for which those 57-inch diameter driving wheels were ideal. Donated to the city of Stillwater, Minnesota, in 1955, this maid-of-all-work is currently operated by the Minnesota Transport Museum.

Western Coal & Coke No 1, another Canadian in exile, was built by Montreal Locomotive Works in 1913 for a coal mining concern in Alberta. Nowadays, No 1 hauls passengers on the Mid-Continent Railway, where its duties sometimes include pulling a snow train. *Below* we see the 4-6-0 piloting a 2-8-2 through the February snow near Devil's Chair, Wisconsin.

The 4-6-2 Pacific

Mystery surrounds the origin of the name 'Pacific.' One theory holds that the 4-6-2 earned the name Pacific when some locomotives of this wheel arrangement were shipped across the Pacific to New Zealand. Another theory suggests that the source is the Missouri Pacific, following delivery of a batch of 4-6-2s to that railroad in 1902. Whatever the origin of the name, the advantages of the Pacific over the Atlantic were its longer boiler and greater horsepower.

Between 1900 and 1930, roughly 6000 4-6-2s were constructed. Many of the engines built for the Harriman-controlled railroads eventually received boosters and larger cylinders, with a resulting increase in tractive power. Though considered pas-

senger locomotives, some Pacifics were pressed into freight service, particularly during the motive power shortages of World War II. Under the United States Railway Association (USRA), formed during World War I to relieve locomotive shortages, a number of standard designs—including light and heavy versions of the Pacific--were constructed for US Railroads.

The Kentucky Railroad Museum's 4-6-2 No 152 is one of the few surviving Louisville & Nashville steam locomotives. Built by Rogers in 1905, the K-1 Class engine now gleams with years of restoration work by museum volunteers. On *these pages*, we see the graceful 4-6-2 traveling the tracks of the 'Old Reliable' once more, with a fantrip from Louisville to Corbin, Kentucky.

Savannah & Atlanta No 750 *(these pages)* originally belonged to the Florida East Coast Railroad. Donated to the National Railroad Historical Society, Atlanta Chapter in 1962, the 1910 Alco became a familiar sight on excursions during the 1960s and 1970s as the Southern Railway steam program gained momentum. Today, the 750 is operated out of Atlanta on specials for the New Georgia Railroad.

The most revered Pacific of all is the legendary Pennsy K4, built in great numbers (425 total) between 1914 and 1928. No 1361 (*these pages*), presented to the city of Altoona, Pennsylvania, and displayed outdoors at Horseshoe Curve for many years thereafter, was restored to operating condition in 1986. Demonstrating the qualities of the entire class—efficiency, dependability and speed—the K4 thunders thorough Julian, Pennsylvania with an excursion. (Photo by John Craft.)

The Pacific type was a favorite with both Canadian transcontinentals, particularly the CPR, and hundreds of them were added to that railroad's roster over the years. CPR Pacific G-3 No 2317 *(below)*, wearing the traditional CPR passenger paint scheme of Tuscan red with gold lining, black and gunmetal grey, was built by the Montreal Locomotive Works in 1923. Purchased by the late Nelson Blount in 1965, it was restored to working order in 1978. Today, No 2317 forms part of the Steamtown collection in Pennsylvania, where it has been repainted black with gold lining and lettering.

The last steam locomotive constructed at the CPR's own Angus shops was G-5a No 1201 *(opposite)*, shown here at Taft, British Columbia, during the Last Spike celebrations of 1985. Normally, the engine resides at the National Museum of Science and Technology in Ottawa. The 1201 powers excursions over a branch line to Wakefield, Quebec, and appears at special rail events in other parts of eastern Canada.

The 4-6-4 Hudson

In Europe, the 4-6-4 was called a Baltic. In the United States, however, the New York Central bestowed the name 'Hudson' in honor of the river that paralleled the railroad's 'water level route.' The 4-6-4 was basically an extended 4-6-2, but the Hudson's four-wheel trailing truck and larger firebox enabled the engine to produce more steam and attain higher speeds than the average Pacific. Over 500 Hudsons saw service in the United States, and 70 in Canada.

The most famous 4-6-4 in the United States was the New York Central's fabulous J3a, a later Alco design of 1937. Some of these engines were given futuristic streamlining and assigned to such premier trains as the *Empire State Express*. Alas, none of the Central's Hudsons were preserved.

In Canada, the CPR used its 65 Hudsons as general service locomotives, and 45 of them were semi-streamlines and named Royal Hudsons after two 4-6-4s hauled King George VI across the country in 1939. Embossed crowns were later fitted to the side skirting. While the restoration of H-le Class Royal Hudson No 2860 under provincial sponsorship in 1974 was a welcome development, authenticity was largely ignored. As a result, the only operating Royal Hudson in Canada was redecorated with plates, plaques and crests. The flaws in 2860's appearance are obvious when one compares the photograph on the *opposite page*, taken near Britannia, with the pre-restoration scene from 1974 *(below)*. No frills or frippery here; just the genuine article. A view from the vestibule *(right)* shows the 4-6-4 climbing through the West Vancouver.

Close to the water's edge, No 2860 *(these pages)* passes Porteau Cove, on the southbound run from Squamish to North Vancouver. CPR enthusiasts can only hope that one day the locomotive will be returned to its original condition and regain some of its lost glory. Perfection, after all, cannot be improved upon.

Heading a special freight jointly sponsored by Steamscenes, Trains Unlimited Tours and the Whistle Stop Hobby Shop of Sacramento, No 28 *(these pages)* turns back the clock. With a plume of smoke that would make an environmentalist shudder, the sprightly 2-8-0 makes yet another movie run-by for the appreciative cameramen.

A full frontal view of No 77 *(opposite)* shows preserved steam as it should be—authentically restored, unspoiled by the bright paint and ornamentation many tourist railroads are convinced will attract the public.

In Mexico, main line steam lingered until 1967, although it was not until recently that Mexico's now dieselized National Railways began to understand the appeal of the steam locomotive. One of the fortunate few to be spared the scrapper's torch is 2-8-0 No 1150 *(below)*, shown here with diesel assistance on an excursion from Mexico City to Tula. Most of Mexico's steam power came over from the United States and No 1150, a 1921 Alco, is no exception.

On the narrow gauge, too, the Consolidation proved to be a reliable workhorse. The Colorado Railroad Museum's Denver & Rio Grande Western C-19 Class 2-8-0 *(these pages)* was 102 years old when this picture was taken in 1983. Sold to a junkyard in 1948, the engine was saved through the efforts of Bob Richardson, the museum curator, who has managed to assemble an impressive collection of steam locomotives, both narrow and standard gauge.

The 2-8-2 Mikado

The two-wheel trailing truck, which helped produce two successful passenger types—the 4-4-2 and the 4-6-2—was also responsible for the most ubiquitous freight engine of all: the Mikado. The first of these were built by Baldwin in 1897 for Japan; hence the name. In the United States, construction began in earnest with the 1904 Alco 2-8-2s supplied to the Northern Pacific. Eventually, the number of Mikados swelled to 10,000. They were used, not only on road work, but on switching chores as well, and many found employment on short lines—logging railroads, for example.

Without question the most famous of all 'Mikes' is Southern Railway Ms Class No 4501, built by Baldwin in 1911. One of the first railroads in the United States to dieselize, the Southern leased back its engine in 1966, to inaugurate what has since become the most impressive program of steam excursions anywhere in the world. Painted in the SR's passenger livery of green with gold leaf, the 4501 is shown (*opposite*) at Meridian, Mississippi, and departing Meridian (*below*) for Birmingham, Alabama. The engine now belongs to the Tennessee Valley Railroad Museum.

Even before playing a leading role in one of the finest railroad movies of all time—*Emperor of the North*—former McCloud River Railroad No 19 *(these pages)* had led a varied and interesting existence. Built by Baldwin in 1915 for an Arkansas short line, the Mike spent some years dodging bullets in Mexico before going to McCloud, California, and then Yreka. During the 1970s and 1980s, the 19 powered excursions on the Oregon, Pacific & Eastern, where parts of the classic about Depression-era hobos were filmed and where this picture was taken. Today, the engine is once again in excursion service on the Yreka Western.

Some Mikados were custom-built for logging railroads. Porter No 5 *(opposite)* went to the Flora Logging Company at Carlton, Oregon, in 1924. The engine had three more owners before being donated to the Western Washington Forest Industries Museum. These days it powers excursions on the Mount Rainier Scenic Railroad at Elbe, Washington.

Another 2-8-2 logger with a varied career is No 2 *(below)*, a Baldwin of 1912 shown switching the Mid-Continent Railway's yard at North Freedom, Wisconsin, prior to heading a snow train. The locomotive is lettered for the company it first served: Saginaw Timber of Keniston, Washington. Subsequent owners included Rayonier, the last logging company in that state to operate conventional rod engines.

So successful was the Mikado type that the USRA designated both light and heavy versions as part of its standardization program. One of the 1266 lightweights used by more than 50 railroads is Nickel Plate Road No 587, shown here getting underway from Frankfort, Indiana, with an excursion returning from Logansport to Indianapolis. Restored by volunteers of the Indiana Transportation Museum, the H-61 was making its first fantrip since retirement in 1955.

One of the newest additions to the growing ranks of active steam locomotives is Cowlitz, Chehalis & Cascade 2-8-2 No 15. A 1916 Baldwin, the engine spent 30 years on display before being given a thorough overhaul by the Mount Rainier Scenic Railroad. Climbing away from Elbe, Washington, beneath a volcanic plume of smoke, No 15 is seen *below* en route to its hometown of Chehalis for a summer of tourist train service with the Chehalis & Centralia Railroad.

In Central America, as in Mexico, US-built steam power in regular service outlasted its cousins north of the Rio Grande. Even as late as 1987, the narrow gauge Railways of Guatemala (FEGUA) had three outside-frame 2-8-2s on hand for emergencies and excursions trains. Paid scant attention by a woman drawing water, No 205 *(below)* thunders through the yard at Escuintla. Yet another Baldwin logging engine is 2-8-2 No 100 *(opposite)* of 1926. First employed by a lumber company in Washington, the locomotive was sold in 1942 to the Santa Maria Valley Railroad, a sugar beet-hauling short line in California, where it spent two more decades. The arrival of diesels rendered No 100 surplus, and it went to a now-defunct tourist operation in Arizona. From 1976 to 1986, the robust Mike enjoyed spells of activity on the Heber Creeper Railroad in Utah.

With Mount Rainier gleaming in the autumn sunlight, Porter No 5 leads a string of skeleton log cars across the Nisqually River Bridge. The ever-popular Mount Rainier Scenic Railroad not only runs passenger trains, but also caters to the whims of enthusiasts as well. A steam-powered logging train—once an everyday sight in the woods of Western Washington—is now a rare event that must be specially arranged.

Few logging railroads remain today. And though the tracks of Rayonier, a company that relied upon steam locomotives into the 1960s, have been torn up in favor of trucks, No 70 (Baldwin 1922) has found a new home on the Puget Sound & Snoqualmie Valley Railroad, located just east of Seattle. The handsome 2-8-8 is shown *below*, approaching a grade crossing near the Snoqualmie depot.

On the slim-gauge tracks of the Rio Grande, the Mikado staged a last stand in the history of the steam locomotive in North America. Though the real show ended in 1968, the whistles of outside-frame 2-8-2s continue to echo in Cumbres Pass and through the canyon of the Animas River. With aspen leaves turning gold in the crisp autumn air, two K-28s *(opposite)* combine forces near Elk Park, Colorado.

At work on both the Durango & Silverton and the Cumbres & Toltec Scenic Railroads are the newer and heavier Mikes of Class K-36. No 481 *(below)*, fitted with a snowplow, waits for an assignment at the Durango roundhouse. Two K-36s *(left)*, silhouetted against the night sky, are ready to roar away from Chama's leading water tower.

Under Rio Grande ownership, the K-36s never appeared on the Silverton branch. However, they did visit Durango on freights from Antonito. The K-28 Class was constructed by Alco in 1923, the K-36 by Baldwin in 1925.

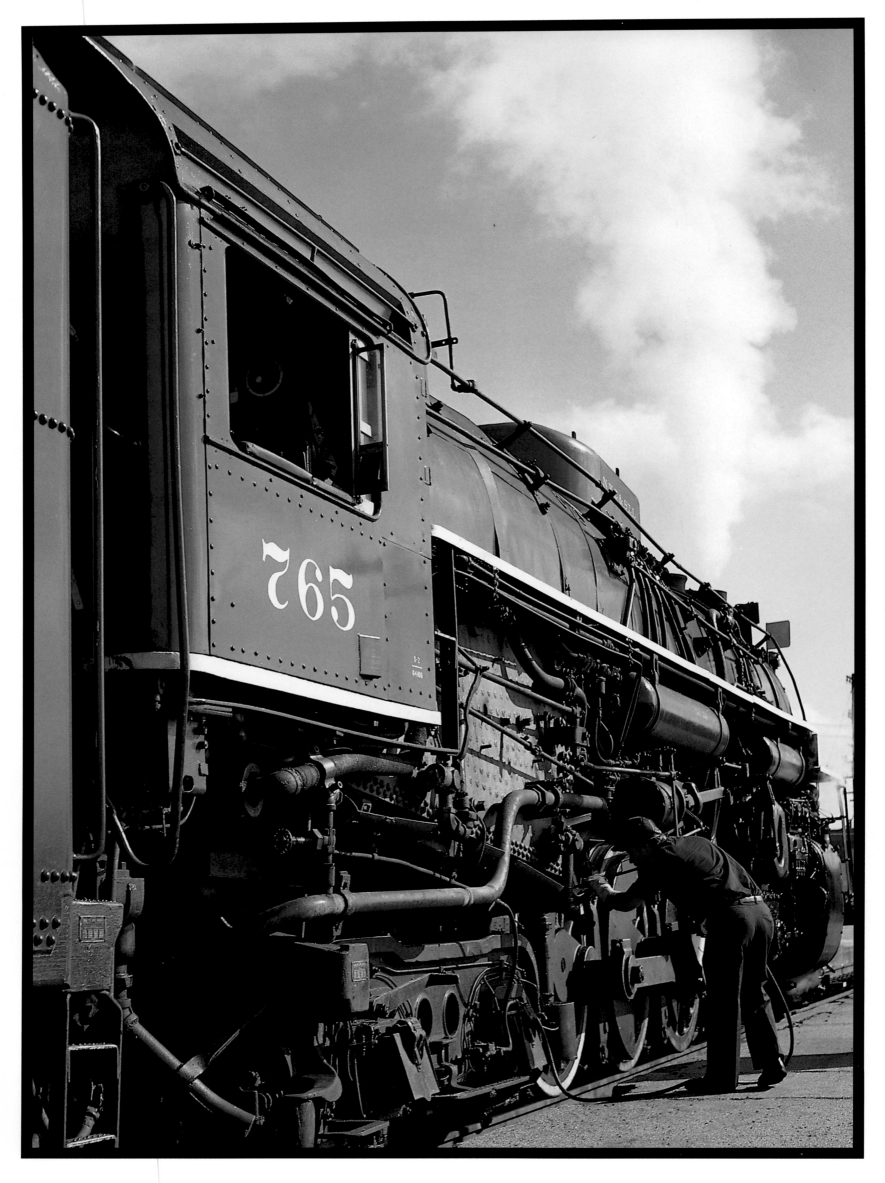

The 2-8-4 Berkshire and the 2-10-4 Texas

The 2-8-4 Berkshire and 2-10-4 Texas types have much in common: they were the first 'superpower' designs developed by the Lima Locomotive Factory. Employing the first four-wheel trailing truck to accommodate a huge firebox, the Berkshires and Texas types could outpull any 2-8-2 or 2-10-2. The locomotive that ushered in the modern superpower steam era in North America was the 2-8-4 Lima built for the Boston & Albany Railroad: the A-1. The A-1 proved that a steam locomotive could combine both power and speed. The Berkshires were named for a mountain range in Massachusetts, where they first entered service on the B & A.

The Nickel Plate Road and fast freight were synonymous. To roll the cars at speed, the railroad ordered 65 S-Class Berkshires between 1942 and 1948. Many NKP 2-8-4s remained at work until 1958, and a number have been preserved, including No 765 *(opposite and right)*, restored by Fort Wayne Historical Society volunteers. Almost identical to the NKP engines were the 2-8-4s of the Chesapeake & Ohio. No 2716 was overhauled by the Norfolk Southern for steam excursions; the Berk *(below)* received its finishing touches at the NS Irondale, Alabama shops. (Photo by Thomas R Schultz.)

Superpower personified: 2-10-4 No 610 was one of Lima's second batch of Texas engines delivered to the Texas & Pacific Railroad in 1927. A beauty this Texan is not, but the huge boiler and firebox, jutting feedwater heater and maze of pipework indicate pure muscle, augmented by a booster for extra power on starting. After accumulating a million miles in freight service between Texarkana and El Paso, the mighty 2-10-4 was donated to the city of Fort Worth. Restored for the Freedom Train in 1976, the 610 spent its next four years as the Southern Railway's most powerful excursion engine. Little of its 98,000 pounds of tractive effort is needed to roll this twenty-car excursion train into Chattanooga's Citico Yard *(these pages)*, but the sight is impressive nevertheless. Five hundred Texas locomotives and 750 Berkshires were produced.

87

Although the 819 was withdrawn in 1955, some of its classmates were transferred west to alleviate a shortage of motive power on its parent company, Southern Pacific. Had the 819 accompanied its classmates to California, it would certainly have been scrapped. Fate was kind to this Cotton Belt 4-8-4. Having managed to avoid the scrapper, the L-1 is still active more than 40 years later. Smoke and steam are the order of the day as the 819 (*below*) sails through Maud, Texas. (Photo by Alan Miller.)

In Canada, Canadian National's 4-8-4, like those in Mexico, were known as Confederations. Smaller than most Northerns in the United States, the CN U-2s were excellent general purpose locomotives. Montreal Locomotive Works constructed the 6218 (*opposite*) in 1942; 30 years later, CN shopped it for excursions in Ontario and the United States. Last operated in 1971, the engine is now displayed at the Fort Erie Historical Railroad Museum.

Built to speed Southern Pacific's new (1937) *Daylight* stream-liner along the scenic Coast Line, the 4449 and its classmates were given a stream-styling and a red, orange and black livery 'as vivid as the California sun.' Where better to view the 4449 and a complete train of Daylight-painted cars than here at Gaviota, California, against the backdrop of the blue Pacific *(these pages)*.

The 4-6-6-4 Articulated

Among North America's most advanced articulateds were the large-boilered Class A 2-6-6-4s of the Norfolk & Western. Like many articulated locomotives built after 1925, these were not Mallets, but standards, employing cylinders of equal size, all working at full boiler pressure. Though intended for fast freight service, the As were often assigned to passenger and troop trains during World War II, and speeds of up to 70 miles per hour were common. Retired in 1960, the 1218 was sold to Union Carbide and used as a stationary boiler. F Nelson Blount, who had saved many engines from the scrapper, purchased the locomotive for his collection in 1965. After being loaned back to the Norfolk & Western, it was overhauled for excursion service in 1987. On one its inaugural 'return to steam' runs, the 1218 *(opposite)* approaches the summit of the Christiansburg grade.

Though not home track for N & W engines, the Rathole Division, between Lexington, Kentucky and Chattanooga, Tennessee, is a popular route with excursionists. In weather all too typical of the region, 1218 *(below)* runs into a downpour near Cumberland Falls.

The highlight of the 1987 National Railroad Historical Society Convention in Roanoke, Virginia was parallel running of both the A Class 2-6-6-4 and the J 4-8-4. In a scene reminiscent of the 1950s, the 1218 restarts a train of empty coal hoppers, while the J prepares to overtake it *(these pages)*.

The 4-6-6-4 Challenger

The Challenger, or 4-6-6-4, was a Union Pacific design, and it seems appropriate that the two survivors belong to that railroad. First introduced in 1936, the UP engines eventually numbered 105, out of a total of 230, which included Challengers built for the Delaware & Hudson; the Northern Pacific; the Spokane, Portland & Seattle; Western Maryland; and Denver & Rio Grande Western. Though intended for general service and in fact capable of wheeling passenger and mail trains at speeds of 70 miles per hour, the 4-6-6-4s were best suited to hauling fast merchandise—which they did until the end of steam on the UP.

No 3985 is one of the later series of UP 4-6-6-4s built by Alco in 1944. The superior performance of these engines was due to good balancing of the side rods and an improved front end to reduce slipping. The 3900s had 14-wheel 'centipede' tenders, restricting their general use to lines west of Cheyenne, Wyoming, where turntables were long enough to accommodate them. Smoke lifters similar to those on the UP Northerns (see pages 100-103) were fitted to 4-6-6-4s assigned to passenger service. The 3985 *(below)* stages a photo run-by east of Laramie, Wyoming.

The most-photographed location in the UP system is Sherman Hill, where Challengers operated until 1959. The 3985 *(opposite, below)* passes Colores, Wyoming, on Sherman's west slope. This rear three-quarter view *(opposite, above)* was taken at Perkins, on the new (1953) third track, used mainly by heavy westbound tonnage.

At Sacramento's Railfair *(below)*, we see a close-up of the big articulated engine, restored by UP employees just in time for the event.

The Shay

Three types of geared locomotives were designed for railroads and branch lines with lightly-laid track, sharp curves and steep grades. The most popular of the three designs was the Shay, built by Lima. On the right side of the locomotive, a three cylinder vertical engine transferred power to two (or three) four-wheel trucks via a geared shaft. To distribute the weight, the boiler was mounted left of center.

The Sierra Railway's No 2 was built in 1922 for the Hutchinson Lumber Company of Oroville, California.

Here, Sierra No 2 *(right)* rides the turntable at Jamestown, California, one of the few locations in North America where the atmosphere of everyday steam railroading remains.

Geared locomotives numbering some 3000 were extensively employed in logging and mining; the Shay type predominated. Pictured *below* are two former loggers—the Pacific Locomotive Association's Pickering Lumber No 12—the oldest (1903) operating Shay in the world—and Clover Valley Lumber No 4. Note the characteristic offset boiler on No 12.

The largest operating narrow gauge Shay in existence is ex-Pickering Lumber No 10 *(opposite)*, which now hauls tourists on the Yosemite Mountain Railway at Fish Camp, California.

Here the three-trucker Sierra No 2 approaches Keystone with one of the Sierra's Wine and Cheese specials.

The Heisler

The Heisler type had two slanting cylinders in a V-shape, one on each side. The cylinders were attached to a crank on a central shaft running along the underside of the boiler to the front and rear trucks, which had side rods and counterweights.

Displayed outdoors for years at Woodland, Washington, the 91 (below) was sold to the Western Forest Industries Museum, Inc

and overhauled for tourist train service at the Mount Rainier Scenic Railroad's shops near Mineral, Washington. Known as a 'West Coast Special,' this engine is one of the largest Heislers ever built.

Mount Rainier Scenic Railroad No 91, originally Kinzua Pine Mills No 102 (opposite), crosses the ex-Milwaukee bridge at Tacoma, Washington.

The Climax

The cylinders on the Climax were mounted high, one on each side of the smokebox. Slanting downward, they were connected to a lateral shaft which drove a main shaft running longitudinally, as on the Heisler.

Ex-Hillcrest Lumber No 10 is also on the Mount Rainier Scenic Railroad's roster. These two views of the 62-year-old engine show it with a train of skeleton log cars near Mineral, Washington *(opposite)* and at the head of a passenger consist on the Nisqually River Bridge *(below)*.

The No 10 was one of the last steam engines to see service on Vancouver Island, British Columbia, where it was used by Hillcrest Lumber until 1969. In 1981, the 10 had the distinction of being the only geared locomotive to appear at the Sacramento Railfair.